I HAVE ARRIVED

Sareeta "Whispers" Lopez

authorHOUSE®

AuthorHouse™
1663 Liberty Drive
Bloomington, IN 47403
www.authorhouse.com
Phone: 1-800-839-8640

First published by AuthorHouse 6/27/2011

ISBN: 978-1-4634-1679-9 (e)
ISBN: 978-1-4634-1599-0 (dj)
ISBN: 978-1-4634-1600-3 (sc)

Library of Congress Control Number: 2011909570

Printed in the United States of America

THIS BOOK WAS CREATED
IN HONOR OF THOSE WHO
WERE AND STILL IS IN DEEP
SUPPORT OF MY TALENT

Past ~ Present ~ Future

Table of Contents

22 POEMS

NOT AS SILLY

You think I'm a silly broad,

Shallow as steal,

But I'm here to tell you I'm real.

You may not know but I'm ready and there's nobody who's got the power to upset me,

Maybe reset me and send me to the next level,

Be ready for me to prove you wrong because I'm about to pedal.

From 2 feet, a bike to self-adjustable leather seats, I'm ready,

You'll be there like the rest of them, throwing confetti.

Brother

Why did you stand there and watch me
struggle?
Any fight we have been through, we have
fought them through our ancestors,
You would rather stick your hands in your
pockets,
Ignoring your sister.
I look at you not because I want to get you
in my bed...
I'm looking to see your soul,
I'm a strong woman but you may be a
weak man,
For your attention, I refuse to beg.
Why do you have a weak mind?
Speak time from way back when slave's
backs used to be what everybody wanted.
Your gestures have haunted me ever since,
Why won't you hold the door for a black
woman struggling?
It doesn't make any sense.

To make my journey easier is what you
would have done but you refused,
Taking me back when I was abused.
Who knew this could have led to strong
emotions?
Black America...still roller coasting.

Addict

Consequences to my actions is what I'm
experiencing.
Sins brought to the surface,
Making a declaration that pay-per-view is
worthless.
No network,
No service.
Blue screens looking back at me,
I needed someone to smack me all the way
back to my great-grandparent's back trees.
While I'm sitting here, miserable, the people
The people that I paid to see is driving
lexus, getting physical.
Look at me!
So sad,
So mad because my favorite shows are on,
I feel like a woman scorn...to hell with
porn!

Sareeta "Whispers" Lopez

YEARN

Automatic tears when I hear how busy you are because I miss

you.

I'm sorry when I hear frustration in your voice,

Time slips away,

Love is a choice and I choose to stay.

You are focused on your work while I'm focused on you,

Clearly seeing things from you point of view.

It's so hard but I have to stiffen up and pull my grown

woman cards.

Pay-per-view is my new addiction but the mission of feeling

complete is incomplete

without you.

PULL UP FROM THE DIRT

Cries, cries

Because she lost the only man she has ever loved,

She remembers what he did to her body but she can't say what love really was.

No substance to it,

Counseling,.. she refused to go through it so,

She cries, failing to realize that she has cried her last tear.

Stronger she's becoming,

Being the leader in battles instead of being a coward and running,

People don't know but it's her self-esteem that God is funding.

Sareeta "Whispers" Lopez

HOTEL ROOM

Rain on her flowers that fills the room with green,

Extensions of her life,

Intensions to walk and live again as a dedicated

mother, lover, wife...in her pot of dreams.

Rain on her as she rains on me,

This job is a blessing but I talked so bad about it,

Shame on me.

Making these hours go by fast with her easy spirit,

I listen for satisfactory,

I'm paying close attention so that I'll be able to hear it.

LOVE AND WAR

Growing and learning,
I'm so glad that I'm taking life by the
horns,
Burning the past that you put down.
It feels good to get away from your grip
because each time
 I talk,
You take me for a trip,
Up and down...it's not that serious.
Love you too to the end of time,
This is called life so,
Please, let me live mine.
You passed on your knowledge so let me
display it,
I never say that I love you,
Bulletproof to protect me,
Detect me with a lie,
Detector but before I do anything,
I pray for confirmation from my protector.
When you say no,
I say yes,
You take the 1st but I choose to second guess.
Set me free because you love me...

Sareeta "Whispers" Lopez

HIS BREED

Growing out of teenage year,
Into maturity,
Teaching our kids the importance of
purity.
Going crazy within our own lives while
keeping them together,
We'll take a stand through any kind of
weather.
Mindless endeavors because we got our
minds fixed on making better lives
For them,
Living half our lives for them.
One blood line runs in all of them.
The fall of them was their father,
Ending the year of toddlers.
Becoming little big people,
Mending each other,
Repenting on random acts of evil.
The oldest, middle and youngest,
For those kids, playing with each other is
the funniest.

Unique traits brings reality
but it's funny when one of them says, "I
know where I'm going,
follow me."
The devil was trying to rip us apart but he
didn't get
Far because we hold the interests of these
beautiful children in our hearts.

THE RITUAL

I got to find comfort in my bed instead of
on this couch,
No need for pain medicine because I can
just sleep this pain out.
Living room or bedroom?
Before the big ritual hits,
I feel like I'm about to have a stroke,
Pain comes from my head and move
quickly to my toes.
My neck,
My back,
The middle of my crack,
Causing me to have gas so bad.
I can't get comfortable
Because the pain is so incredible,
Nothing looks edible!
Everything is plastic!
Pain is long lasting but tomorrow,
It will shrink and won't be so massive.
I can't wait!

THE DANCE

Forgetting how I can have so much fun dancing,

Romancing you, expressing how I really feel about you.

When I stop,

Your mouth is open

Because you didn't know I can dance like that.

You like that...when I dance and sweat,

Giving you something that you will never forget.

I love you so much.

I always want to surprise and not disappoint,

You should know by now that my love is on point.

Sareeta "Whispers" Lopez

SECRET LIFE

Hurting inside because of what you said…
You couldn't be with me because you
thought I would set you up,
I never thought I could regret that time we
sexed each other up.
I don't know how to come toward you,
Punish or reward you,
You can afford me but can I afford you?
Why did I allow myself to become a slave
for you?
What if we went through that again?
Would you still think I was setting you
up?
It becomes a sticky situation,
Misty condensation,
A one way conversation: I want to share
this moment with you.
It wasn't my fault because I doubled up on
birth control,
You can't blame me because I had no
control.

I had an abortion to prove the pregnancy
wasn't on purpose,
I never really gotten over it,
In fact, it's still hurting.

WHAT THEY WANT FROM ME?

Why are they coming back?
To see how I would react?
Why did I see him in the same
parking lot
That I was in,
2 spots from me?
Looking stupid, short and funny.
He didn't want me when he had me,
Let me guess...
When we were together, he was doing
me dirty?
Why is this dude calling?
Stalling and wasting my time?
I put him on the reject list so he won't
be able to get through
To my line.
I hope this isn't a set up to get me
killed
Because the whole time,
I kept it real.

What they need to do is line up all
their feelings for me and go on a
killing spree.
They lost a grown woman and they're
recognizing it years later...
And why is this 10 minutes and 2
months later?
He won't ever get close to my son or
close to anyone
I have connections with,
He made his bed,
Now, he has to lay in it-by himself.

Sareeta "Whispers" Lopez

ALMOST OUT OF TIME

I feel cheated,

Blocked,

Put on the clock but little does he know I'm falling

Apart at the seams.

I need him to give me time before he ignores me again.

I feel cheated,

Mistreated like a mistress,

I never thought I'd have to receive this.

Sad and broken,

My heart is open but he just closed me out of his,

I have someone else but whose attention would I rather have?

HIS!!!

BRING ME BACK

I need a time to heal,
Kill these demons,
Fast and anxious like semen.
I hate when I forget where I'm at,
Act with emotion,
I'm catching sickness as this boat is
waddling on the ocean.
Just a toddle at this game,
Would give any amount of dollars to have
your last name.
I need to win back what the inside of me
now lacks,
Stacks of paper I see coming to me,
But at the same time avoiding thin cracks
that promises
 to bring death
To me.
I don't want him to screw me anymore,
I want you,

Sareeta "Whispers" Lopez

there's evidence that I've done more damage
to myself than I've done to you.
Dismiss me from this block and bring me
closer,
I'm wishing on a star tonight like it's my
4 leaf clover.

I'M GONE

You're going down but he's coming up,
It's us that I'm summing up.
One time and after that,
Nothing seemed the same but there was
nothing to hold onto except physical gain.
The balance that I had is tipping,
It's me that I'm whipping because you
weren't worth it.
Nice,
Many hopes but it's him that I'm
having many strokes over.
Not cheating anymore even though the
eating
Was Incredible.
I wanted much more but I don't feel right,
Out the door.
Conversations were slipping,
What was I sipping?
Why would I depend on you?
Even when I ask you for your input,
Nothing come through,
Don't care what you do just don't talk to
me.

Sareeta "Whispers" Lopez

SIDE SWIPPED

They're gone,
They forgot about me...
For dealing with them,
I was dead wrong.
I thought I would feel better by releasing
them,
His job was to increase so I could win but
instead,
I feel empty,
Those feelings became more toxic the longer
they're in me.
One relationship like how it was supposed
to be,
I'm hurting and the pain is shooting right
through me.
Forever is gone,
For believing them, I was wrong,
A heartbreaker never breaks even,
I'm allergic to bullshit but I keep going
back
To the lies though I can't stop sneezing.

LATE NIGHTS

After the candles are blown out and the
lights are turned off,
I'm burnt out but it's hard to sleep.
I wrote a lot,
Hoping that rest is the only thing that
would creep up on me.
Slave to whatever my life throws at me.
Braiding and under grading my success,
I would feel 100% complete if only if I got
some rest.
Shopping bags but not under my eyes,
In my hands,
Dreaming of peace were in my plans,
But they refuse to happen.
Can't stand this,
I thought I ran this but it's feeling like I'm
someone's dog bitch.

Sareeta "Whispers" Lopez

OXYMORON

Letting go of these dark butterflies of slavery,

I feel free beyond the hurt I dispensed to the people I love.

Every layer of pain that I react to causes me to fall into those habits

That I defeated in the past,

I allow this pain to last.

Stopping when I get to question if my action are worth it,

My time,

I served it but for some unknown reason I keep going back,.

Not accepting that that season is over.

MY REASON FOR BREATHING

I don't want to lose him so, I hold on
tighter,
He my little boy,
The time we enjoy can never be found
except deep inside my heart,
He's turned my life from a black canvas to
a work of art.
I can't imagine waking up, knowing he's
not here,
He defines me with seasoning,
Has turned my thinking into reasoning.
He's my everything...
Without him,
I would not have found love,
Without him, I wouldn't know what being
a protector was,
Lectures were not to get pregnant but I'm
glad I did.
I don't want to share him because that will
be more distance between us,
I trust that he'll remember the good times
we had,

Sareeta "Whispers" Lopez

He's the best someone I ever had...I'm more
of a father to him than his dad.
I want him to remember when we laughed,
Cried when we were sad,
Life without him would be bad.
He's my reason for breathing.

FUZZY

I don't know what I'm going to do but I know
that
For now, I'm doing two.
It's a lot that I'm putting my body through.
Can't let go of none of them but I know I'll have
to choose one soon,
I'm so consumed with lust...
What happens to you, me, both of us?
People get beat and killed for this,
Am I not mature enough for this?
I don't need to take a break because he'll find
someone else,
I'll need more than mental help...medication,
To be assisting me would be daily meditation.
Broken dreams,
Broken hearts, broken glass and metal on the
ground that came from a couple of cars.
I can't sleep because my mind is not made up,
I'm human-created which means that I was born
to fuck,
Can't trust situations will be straight after I cut
ties because
Karma will penetrate herself right through my
pours,
I'll be a slave to my cheating like a dog on all
fours.

Sareeta "Whispers" Lopez

I am a slave,
Hoping for better days but until that day came,
I'll take this to my grave.
Back and forth,
Begging for someone to come and take this
torch
Before I burn my future to the ground,
We'll turn from each other for a minute but I
fear
So much that he won't turn back around.

MINE!

Hot boy,

My toy,

Today, I said bye-bye to them other boys.

He brings me the goodies,

Cheat on me, would he?

I think not,

I think he's hot, he's everything to me that they're not.

Kisses my feet because I'm his queen,

This time comes two times: pass by in my lifetime and in my dreams.

MAGIC

I can except if you're in jail better than if
You were in another woman's arms,
Wake up call,
Sound the alarm because it's time to move
on.
I lost a yearlong battle,
Our last phone call went from you
apologizing to
You putting the saddle on me,
Saying some crazy things,
Turned on me like a pit bull, call me
names\.
You couldn't take the pressure...
You took it out on me.
You were trying to tenderize me but you
were
The one done,
You?
I don't want none.
That's how you are ending this?
I can't believe it,
You have worked hard for this opportunity
Now, you're going to leave it?

Frustrated but not at me,
Don't even come back to me because you
burnt your bridges,
You can't even earn your way back.
You went backwards,
To rags from riches but you know what?
I send my best of wishes!

INTRODUCTION

MY JOURNEY BEFORE ARRIVING

The inspiration for writing

came at the age of 15 years old when I realized that my best emotion came out in poetry. I was a sophomore in high school and was a dedicated fan of rap music which had watered the seed that God put inside of me. At the time, I didn't know what my talent was but I knew that I couldn't stop writing. Whether it was on notebook paper, napkins, or my hands, my words were written down.

One day in study hall, I

got a strong urge to write a poem on the teacher's chalkboard. I was surprised that the teacher and students embraced the words that I wrote. Soon after, the teacher had designated a spot on the board just so that my talent could be displayed. My poem was not allowed to get erased until I replaced it with a new one. I was not aware that my ability for writing was so great until my English teacher told me how emotional she was after reading some of what I wrote. Right after, a friend and classmate of mine suggested that I write a book.

For many years, I struggled with the idea of being a successful author because I had difficulties with my confidence. But as myself-esteem crumbled, my poetry gained strength. Writing became a source of therapy for everything I went through. When I came home from school, I would lock myself in my room, turn the music up and start writing.

After twelve years, I have decided to write a book because I want to share my poetry with people who appreciate this form of art. This book was also created to test the durability and impact of my talent.

I hope the same joy I got writing
this book would find itself in your
spirit as you read my poems.

Thank you for your support!

LOVE AT LAST

I GOT BETTER LOVE

Fate,

Real, not fake,

Determination is what love takes,

Efforts is what I have to make and when he sees me, the expressions will quickly change on his face.

When I'm in search for him, things come to me that we haven't did,

Emotional pulls now got me because now, I'm having dreams of someday having his kids.

Faith and determination is all that I have,

You can't push me down and expect me not to react,

Class is what other females lack,

I can kiss him and it's guaranteed that he'll kiss a thousand times back.

I STILL

I'm still in love.

I still fiend for you,

I still want to be caressed and undressed by you.

When I let you go,

I'm trying to push you away,

I don't want to disappointment to find me, I really want to stay.

Time alone seem so far away,

I'm very happy you schedule me in your day.

Today, I blew wishes up in the sky but I know one of two things: they can choose to or refuse to fly.

They don't know because I continue to carry the weight discretely,

I will be reminded every time to put your love back neatly.

A divorce...it's like that,

I'm not letting her take you away from me,

When she bites me, I'll bite back.

ALWAYS LOVE

I can't understand but I'm trying to,

Seeing you, dying to.

It's not what you did but how you did it,

I want to forgive and forget it.

Before any of us separate from this life,

I want you to know that I appreciate the good

and bad times we shared...I'm sorry.

CLOSED EYES

Don't wake me because I'm dreaming of the one I love,

I realized that my fantasies can be anything.

He touches me in my dreams and I melt as though it's reality.

Smiles come to my face because this is a pleasurable place.

I get butterflies,

We got it back the way it used to be,

We dance all over the floor and everyone in the world is climbing on each other just to witness you and me.

I realize that reality is nothing but a breath away but I still would like to dream,

You don't get that I'm enjoying myself without the other females,

Don't wake me,

I don't want to go through fighting over you again so don't make me.

Promise that you will be in my dreams forever...

I miss the person that you used to be because the toughest

fights were fought together.

DREAM OPPERTUNITIES

It's your complexion that has gotten me in a frenzy,

I would move you in and spoil you with my love,

Just don't befriend me.

If we had problems,

I wouldn't run away,

Instead, I would want to stay and work hard until everything was again ok.

If you're worth it, you will love me more and walk through every door.

You are beautiful,

Sexy black and curly is your hair,

Next time I go to 31 flavors, I pray that you are there.

I promise if you're worth it,

You'll get the full understanding of what I stand for,

Other guys took me for granted,

I fell in love before but didn't plan it,

He was the one I couldn't stand with, I had the supplies but he didn't demand it.

YO-YO

The thing that makes me so thankful
for you is that no matter how sunny or
cloudy outside,

No matter if I look good or bad,

You're always willing to be around me.

In the middle of it all,

You hold my hand, whatever it takes to
make it through, you do.

Somehow, you can always tell that I'm
slipping into my zone,

Showing me that there is no reason to feel
alone.

Before I start getting attached, I leave but I
cry more,

my dreams about love come true but they
die more.

I love you with each day that passes,

Damn! I didn't know your love for me
would last.

I'm sorry for running away from your acceptance,

Separation is my answer for everything for

everything but by the end of the day, I'm alone,

Respect from you is what I'm afraid of because

it might turn into control or rejection.

You're the third person that's been through the fire with me but the first one that I haven't lost in the process.

ALL IN ME

With the love this is all in me,

I give you the chance to see

That loving you is all in me.

Through all things and ways of life,

The one thing that will carry us through

is love.

I could talk about love forever and ever,

Like the birds of the feather,

Or the birds and the bees: loving you is all
in

me.

Believe that love has something good in
store

For you so, just have patience.

Sometimes, love doesn't make any sense
but

That is what trust is for.

MIND, BODY AND SOUL

My heart is a place where

I keep everything deep,

It's where lies, secrets, and feelings

Are embedded in me.

Seductions exposed along with it's

Hiding places,

Uncertain passions go round and round,

Going in constant mazes.

I can't control my feelings

More than you can control yours,

Right now, I feel passion,

Later, I may feel more.

I'm 17yrs old, I can't be in love yet,

I still have a lot of time to think about

That stuff, I must not forget.

Sareeta "Whispers" Lopez

HOPE

Hoping we can work things out,

I'm not understanding but I'm trying hard to figure you out.

What makes me love you more?

A chemical balance between us or the fact that there is more trust?

From me to you, here's a kiss for the next storm that we go through.

I'm feeling more comfortable but I'm not sure,

Just keep in mind that once upon a time, I was his but now I'm forever yours.

Tonight is beautiful but my great-grandmother is missing,

If only I could tell you how good it felt when it was my hand that she was kissing.

I miss your voice and what you said to me that night,

I wish we were still in the same position because it felt just right.

I miss you because nobody else can make it better,

The pain and struggle,

There's no one that could face it better...

It's good to know that my great-grandparents are finally in heaven together.

A SPECIAL MOMENT IN TIME

He taught me how to be steady in hectic

Situations,

He talked to me and gave me comfort on
occasions

But he's missing now.

I used to be head over hills when I spotted
either one of his cars but I have realized
that I have to leave this as "done".

The New York rain hit us with a
sentimental value that can never be
explained,

Little did I know that hi absence would
cause my head some major pain.

Oluwayemisi would come to see me,

Never sexual but always respectable.

The time in New York wasn't enough because it's him that

my family didn't trust but I prayed for confirmation, it was

a go and for that one special moment, it was all about us.

Sareeta "Whispers" Lopez

NEVER AGAIN

Yeah, I still think about you,

Yeah, I'm still loving you-from a distance because you have pushed me away. It's the compassion for my fragile heart that you lack,

There's another reason for me not to pay attention to you,

Why should I try to talk when it's easier to show my back?

Why should I answer your calls If you're going to disrespect me, acting like a fool?

You must have forgotten that I let you borrow my car the days that I was in school,

I realized that I wasn't headed in love's direction,

I don't understand why you stopped giving affection,

You threatened me but I'm not stupid because I know that I still have your protection.

You are going through a lot but that doesn't mean my life stops,

Even if I wanted to, I refuse to freeze the clock.

I can't be there for you at all now,

You lied to set me up but I'm slowly making a rebound.

Knocking me out my corner was the best thing you did.

You're suffering...

Meanwhile, I'm chilling, doing me, having a chance to live.

CHANCE IT

You're shy and I understand,

You came to me like a better man,

For me, I don't know what you have planned but we will find out.

Yesterday, I don't know why I got bad nerves but when I saw how determined you were, I got a buddle of nerves.

I don't want you to back away from me,

You should let me love you,

I promise I'll never make you cry,

Or make you feel like you should pass me by.

I'm wondering about you and I know you're wondering about me too so let me let you know right now that I'm going to stay true.

Your eyes dropped as they rose again,

After the little conversation we had, I didn't even have to ask 'why' again.

HAVE MERCY

It's with him that the faded pictures came back into view,

I wasn't expecting to see him ever again but then, I felt new.

My soul's pair,

I felt happy as if nothing else mattered for the one minute,

I never knew that my heart was so much in this.

For days, I asked God to bring him to me,

Yes, I laid low for a couple of weeks,

Now, I finally see that all this time was worth it,

I saw a man standing in front of me who seemed so perfect,

This could be a lie but I'm starting to get the feeling that besides my son, he's my purpose.

Sareeta "Whispers" Lopez

His features are luxurious.

From the slight slant in his eyes to his masculine form I had in mind,

Love has carried over into me from the start to the end of time.

I asked God to have mercy on me because I was at the end of my peak,

It was the process of loneliness' that I didn't want to repeat.

I can tell that he's a good man,

Yes, he has a lot going on but who doesn't?

I feel that I am here to show compassing, trying to understand.

DISEASE

I need you to kiss my lips,

I cry to myself when I hear the name 'precious', that's what you used to call me because I was easy to break.

I'm still in love with you,

Those times of denying,

Late night, I would catch myself lying for you.

Time,

Patience,

What's killing me is the waiting.

I can't explain it...

My feeling for you are dangerous because I'll do just about

anything.

The deficit of my disease is four times the depth of the ocean,

There were only nine bottles on the shelf because I drank the

tenth potion.

LONELY ONE

A penny for his thoughts,

It's simply what I was taught.

I can't believe this long is how much I fought.

Write what I'm thinking-what's happening is that my heart is sinking.

I walk around with tissues,

Spreading around your issues and simply throwing you away.

Now, my life is good,

Have you learned anything from me?

Have I learned anything from you?

Yeah, in this life I have to be strong toward each and every view.

I can't lock my feelings from you,

I can no longer hide from you.

All I can do is lie to you,

It makes me wonder what would it be like for you if I died.

Would you try and make it?

If the opportunity came around, would you take it?

Time is passing.

Your one and only love,

Your baby is who she is having.

9 centimeters to go...

Tears and laughter is what we had but if you're not going to step up, I'm not either, I'll just go date someone else and let the opportunities with you pass.

I HAVE
RECOGNIZED
MY WORTH

SO GRIMMY

Don't do me anymore favors,

I've been chewing for so long that our relationship has lost its' flavor.

Don't be so dopey when you hear that others want to get to know me.

Everything you lost was because you are a P.O.S,

You're just mad because you realized that you have lost the best,

If you want to keep me, don't ever put me through those disrespectful tests.

Don't do me any favors by calling yourself walking back into my life because you will be walking back with a new complexion after I finish smacking you with this ray of light.

I can't believe you are the one I wanted to get with,

Man! I should have learned when you broke your first 2 promises.

LET IT GO

Out of sight,

Out of mind,

I hate the moments when I run out of time.

Aggravation is what I'm dealing with because everybody has my number and it's making me sick.

How long?

Too long!

I came into this thing head strong,

But I came to the realization that this is a dead song.

I'm mad and it's sad because I came into this with an open heart but it's closed now,

Don't ride this ride because it's officially closed down.

Out of sight,

Out of mind but you know what?

I'm not holding my tongue next time!

Sareeta "Whispers" Lopez

A Step Back

I look at you and wonder what kind of threat

Are you really under?

I'm scared for you...

He places his friends before you.

If you don't this guy around, it's done,

I had my suspicions,

I have never met someone who is better than everyone.

My beauty is being forgotten because I see you hurting and at times, I see you bleed,

I'll let him go because I can see that it's more of my affection that you need.

LAY DOWN

You made your bed now, lay in it,

You wanted someone else with a sweet spot now, play in it,

I would help you out but it wouldn't be right,

You wouldn't listen to me and I realized that I have to let you go through what we call "life".

It's supposed to be 50/50,

Not 90/10, 80/20,

I'm not yours yet but you keep on bragging as though you have already won me.

You made your bed in the dark with a girl still in there,

I thought more of us but I guess it's called life because nothing is fair.

I have noticed a difference in your scent,

I noticed that you stress a lot more,

Smelling like you are still bent,

You threw me away and I'm staying away,

Walking in the other direction when I see you passed out on the marble floor.

The Way I Feel

I just thought you were finish
playing me for a fool

I thought you were done breaking
my concentration during the
hours of school.

I can't hear from you but you
demand answers which isn't cool.

I just thought I would be your wife
someday but how can I when you
made this street one way?

I don't like it when you treat me
this way.

I am furious but no longer curious
because you left me with a seed to
harvest myself,

I am furious because you told
me that I would be yours forever
but instead our relationship has
withered away,

I thought we would be together but
instead, I am here to work while
you choose to play.

Lately, my feeling clash when I
think of you,

But I realize that soon enough I
would be in the past, on the brink
from you.

ENOUGH

"Back Talk" follows me and allow me to be take what

has been stolen from me by this "numb nut" who left me

here in the cold,

I'm sitting out here with my baby,

Realizing that he is definitely out of my life

But all I feel like doing is hitting him with my bike,

From front to back,

Left to right.

My car, he took,

Stole my self-esteem out its' glass box like a filthy crook.

Saying the things he said to hurt and disrespect me,

Now, I take it by force, getting stronger in moments that he has neglected me,

Practicing on telling him "no",

Not letting that soft exterior show because that is what he took advantage of,

I have advance love and extended within myself,

Loving me, Helping me, making love my wealth.

BREAKING POINT

My friends,
My child's father,
His mom,
Why did she even bother?
What the hell is she thinking of?
Wanting to get information from me for
the one she loves but I refuse to tell her
anything,
Many things that she wants to know but
I'm not telling her.
I've handled the pressure this time because
I have been through this before, I've been
praying for this to be over but eventually
God will shut this window and open
another door.
Knowing that I'm second has got me
checking but why do I stay if I'm being
disrespected?
I might as well leave this scene and let it
remain as collapsed wreckage.

Sareeta "Whispers" Lopez

DENIAL

How can you look at me like there is nothing wrong?

This has been turned into the last song.

I show love and compassion but he don't appreciate it,

I write these kinds of poems even though I hate it but it leads me to believe that you all are related.

You don't see the anguish you put me through comes back to you but you don't seem to know what I'm talking about,

I have no doubts that it will come back to you ten times as hard,

From finish to start,

I hope every girl plays you out,

I'm waiting for the day when someone finally leaves you out,

Forget my number in turn because I finally threw yours out.

I'M MISSING YOU, BABY

SLUMPED OVER

When I woke up without you tucked in
my womb,
I stayed up night and day, crying in
my room.
I could still feel your strength in me.
I was too scared witness how much
harder life would be through the years,
I wasn't convicted that I would have
fewer tears and to surrender to the fact
that you were gone,
So many rights but this made life all
wrong,
I play music occasionally and sing to
you in song.
I've seen your spirit and hear your
voice,
See you walking with your big brother,
I could have made a better choice but it's
all done now but I always want you to
know that I love you.

PAINFUL MEMORIES

5 months and 26 days,

I remember when I 1st heard about you being taken away.

I used to go to you for laughs and to say I love you,

My blood existed because of you.

I swear I hear you talking to me.

I hear you in the halls or so I thought,

Holding onto the things that you taught me,

I feel your presence,

Almost like you are walking toward me.

I move like a thief in the night,

The way that you might,

You changed the way I look at the world,

Family, friends and life.

27 Days In October

The worst day of my life,
Rain comes down harder,
I hear sirens and in the distance, there are
flashing lights.
My baby is being taken away,
My soul has already passed away.
I saw myself at 9 months,
Happy and free with my partner kissing
me.
Now, both frames of mind are distorted,
messed up,
Day 27 in October started this cycle of bad
luck.
I'm crying as though you were born
already,
my energy is gone,
I'm feeling like the fight is over,
my eyes feel heavy.
You would have been born in the summer,
instead of saying yes and staying, I
should have said no, remaining pure but
this is the price that's brought on by sex.

I'm fighting hard to keep you but reality
is slowly seeping through,
My choices are gone about keeping you.
I hate to admit it but you can't come yet
because I'm barely taking care of myself
and my studies for school are not done yet.

Sareeta "Whispers" Lopez

DON'T WANT TO

How can people tell me to kill my baby?
1st, they are happy for me,
now they turn into monsters, acting all
crazy.
This is the hardest month to deal with
because
I'm going through so many changes-
biological and
Emotions,
More than ever, I'm feel down,
An abortion?! That's not how I get down.
It's not going to happen,
People are steady telling me to do it but for
better or worse,
I'm going through this.
Storms and stress is what my pregnancy
be like,
I'm trying to see my baby's smile but I'm
still waiting for God to say, "Let There Be
Light",

I'm hearing people tell me that in a couple more years, it will be right, I'm young so that makes people believe that I'm ignorant and can't see right, I prayed for this moment so I know it's got to be right.

SO SICK

I got to make myself eat, sleep and laugh
because I don't want to do anything-I'm
missing you.
I don't want to stop crying,
My choice would be lying here and waiting
on you but time goes on.
This week I'm supposed to be on vacation
but I'm feeling so depressed...I thinking
I'm going to need some medication.
I never thought I could feel this way,
Nights that my son is gone,
For your calls, I pray but I need to accept
that the fact that you are permanently out
of my life.

NATURE TOOK IT'S COURSE

Am I bad for letting stress get to my baby?

I prayed, received but didn't take care of it.

Am I a bad person?

I'm down, looking up to my blessings, watching them fly away,

I have been stressing,

But allowing the emotionally have cleansing on the day-2-

day basis.

I look back and agree that I was a bad person,

God granted me a dream but I didn't nurture it so nature to

it's course.

SEARCHING

I want to hold you,
Kiss you,
Thinking of you every second because I
miss you.
Every morning I'm mourning that you are
not hear,
I don't need money,
All I want is you,
Since your disappearance, I've shed a lot of
tears.
What If?
Those are the questions but where the heck
are the answers?
This lost is the worst because it's getting at
me like a curse,
Cancer.
Will I ever see what the two of you look
like?
Just for ten minutes I just want to cross
over to the other side. I'm missing you so
bad, It's a chance with you that I wish I
had.

About the Author

Sareeta Lopez is a single mother on the way to making a name for herself. The experiences that she has had become her best teacher in life. Her first book, "I Have Arrived", has been one of the most rewarding things she has ever done next to taking care of her son. 13 years in the making!

Thank You's

GOD- YOU ARE MY PERFECT PEACE WHEN EVERYTHING IS CRAZY. THANK YOU FOR GIVING ME THIS TALENT AND ALLOWING ME TO FIT INTO A WORLD THAT IS SO DYNAMIC. THANK YOU FOR LEADING ME THE WAY TO SO MANY OPPERTUNITIES THAT I THOUGHT I MISSED.

MY MALYCHI- THANK YOU FOR BEING THE VOICE OF REASON AND THE REASON WHY I BREATHE. I'M SO HAPPY THAT GOD INTRODUCED US BECAUSE YOU HAVE BEEN MY MOTIVATION FOR LIVING LIFE. I COULDN'T IMAGINE MY LIFE WITHOUT YOU!

MOM & GRANDMA ELLIE- THANK YOU FOR BEING THE SINGLE MOTHER THAT YOU WERE AND FOR NEVER LEAVING ME ALONE, YOU TAUGHT ME THE VALUE OF BEING A WOMAN IN THIS WORLD. THANK YOU FOR GIVING ME AN OPPORTUNITY TO GET A BETTER EDUCATION AND LIFE.

GRANDPA ART AND GRANDPA RANDY- THANK YOU FOR BEING THE MEN IN MY LIFE THAT I NEEDED AND STILL NEED TIL THIS DAY. YOU TAUGHT ME HOW I

SHOULD RECEIVE RESPECT FROM A MAN. THANK YOU FOR BEING MY CRUTCH WHEN I FELT LIKE LIFE WAS PASSING ME BY.

MR SYLVESTER- THANK YOU FOR COMING INTO MY LIFE AS A MAN OF ENCOURAGEMENT AND LOVE. YOU HAVE REALLY SHOWED ME THE REASON WHY FATHERS EXISTS.

GRANDMA EDNA-THANK YOU FOR BEING THERE WHEN I NEEDED SOMEONE TO TALK TO. THE MOMENTS OF LAUGHTER MEANT SO MUCH TO ME.

DAD-THANK YOU FOR PASSING THIS WONDERING TALENT ONTO ME. YOU HAVE TAUGHT ME THE MEANING OF COMMUNICATION IN SO MANY WAYS THAT I CAN'T BEGAN TO DESCRIBE.

 TO ALL OF MY FAMILY: YOU HAVE WATCHED ME GROW AND TURN INTO THIS WOMAN IS   APPRECIATING LIFE SO MUCH MORE. YOUR LOVE AND ENCOURAGEMENT HAS GOTTEN ME THROUGH SOME ROUGH TIMES BUT ALSO, GUIDE ME THROUGH WHERE DAYS ARE ALSO EASY.

I REALLY ENJOY BEING IN THIS LIFE SO I COULD MEET WONDERFUL PEOPLE SUCH AS: MICHAEL HALL, RICK WATSON (THE 2ND VOICE OF REASON IN MY LIFE), AUTHOR T REAL AND AUTHOR JEWELZE (FOR LETTING ME REHERSE MY POETRY ON THEIR BLOG TALK RADIO SHOW), AUTHOR VERONICA BLACKBERRY (FOR ALLOWING ME TO COME INTO

YOUR WORLD. MIMI BROWN, SERENA SOL BROWN, AND PATTI JACKSON (FOR ALLOWING ME TO GET CLOSE ENOUGH TO YOU TO WITNESS WHAT LEGENDS ARE.

LAST BUT NOT LEASE, THANK YOU TO MONIQUE AVERRETTE. EVER SINCE I MET YOU, YOU HAVE BEEN AN INSPIRATION. THANK YOU FOR LETTING ME KNOW THAT I CAN BE ANYTHING I WANT TO BE. LOVE YA, GIRL!

*Special appreciation to Author House for helping me get to the finish line.